# Gothick
# HERTFORDSHIRE

### Jennifer Westwood

## Shire Publications Ltd

# Contents

Printed in Great Britain by C. I. Thomas & Sons (Haverfordwest) Ltd, Press Buildings, Merlins Bridge, Haverfordwest, Dyfed SA61 1XF.

British Library Cataloguing in Publication Data:
Westwood, Jennifer.
Gothick Hertfordshire.
1. Hertfordshire — Visitors' guides.
I. Titles. 914.25'804858.
ISBN 0-7478-0041-3.

# Acknowledgements

I am indebted to a number of people and institutions for professional assistance generously given: Berkhamsted School for Boys; Alan Fleck of Hitchin Museum; Libby Hall of Hemel Hempstead Public Library; David Johnson of Watford Public Library; Debbie Wardle of Cheshunt Central Library; and, as ever, Peter Walne, the County Archivist. I would also like to acknowledge the cheerful co-operation of the staff of the National Westminster Bank, Stevenage; the publican, T. J. Ashcroft, and those before and behind the bar of The Steamcoach, Hemel Hempstead; Pam Rutherford and the publican, Stephen Norrie, of The Red Lion, Digswell Hill; and the publican, Douglas Tyler, of The White Horse, Burnham Green. Special thanks, for going out of their way to be helpful, are due to Sophie Piebenga, Head Gardener at Knebworth; Alan Smith, of the Friends of Layston Church; and Jack Reynolds, Parish Clerk and Verger of Northchurch — a mine of information. Thanks also to Margaret Hole and David Perman. To all these helpful people I am most grateful.

Illustrations are acknowledged as follows: J. W. Chandler, pages 8, 13 (upper), 15 (upper), 19 (upper), 20 (right), 29 (lower), 35 (lower), 41, 48; Fiona French, page 42 (lower); Cadbury Lamb, pages 6, 7, 9, 10, 11, 13 (lower), 15 (lower), 17, 18, 19 (lower), 20 (left), 22, 25, 26, 28, 29 (upper), 30, 32, 33 (upper), 34, 35 (upper), 38, 39, 42, 49, 50; Jeffery Whitelaw, page 14. The cover picture is by Grahame Tomkins. The map is by Robert Dizon.

# Introduction

Hertfordshire, one of England's smallest counties, is a place of contrasts and surprises.

The traveller often comes to it expecting to find commuter suburbs, New Towns and Garden Cities. So he does. Yet at the same time he discovers as narrow and leafy lanes, as picturesque ancient houses and village greens, and as many survivals of a past over but not forgotten — lock-ups and gibbets, stocks and whipping-posts — as anywhere in England. Perhaps more — for the London overspill that has altered Hertfordshire has in many places also acted as a preservative.

The overspill began with the Romans, who drove great roads through the county, marched along them, settled beside them. Later, these same roads brought footpads and highwaymen to prey on passing travellers, from the notorious Dick Turpin to the Wicked Lady.

Because it was convenient to the Court, Hertfordshire abounded in palaces, great houses and great monasteries, and has been the scene of dark deeds and skulduggery at the highest levels. Its traditions present a microcosm of English history: the Knights Templar, the Great Plague, the murder of Charles I, the Rye House Plot, the Monmouth Rebellion.

At the same time it was a farming county supplying London, and even today the north-east and the Chiltern parishes remain deeply rural. Here were long-preserved old ways of thinking and old traditions. It is no accident, perhaps, that Hertfordshire had both the last person condemned to death for witchcraft and the last highwayman hanged in England.

# Using this book

The numbers preceding the directions at the end of each entry are sheet numbers and grid references for Ordnance Survey Landranger maps. Road numbers and names, and street names are as given in the *Ordnance Survey Hertfordshire Street Atlas* (George Philip, 1986). Opening times of houses and gardens mentioned as being open to the public can be found in *Historic Houses, Castles and Gardens Open to the Public* (British Leisure Publications, published annually). Place-names printed in bold type in the text are cross-references to other entries.

# Gothick
# HERTFORDSHIRE

### Places mentioned in the gazetteer

BEDFORDSHIRE

Ickle
Pirton
Wayting Hill

Temple
Dinsle

Whitwe

Gubblecote

Markyate
Cell

Devil's Dy

Aldbury
Tring

Little
Gaddesden

Redbourn

Nomanslan

Northchurch • Frithsden
Grim's
Ditch

• Berkhamsted
Bourne End

• Piccotts End

St Alba

Boxmoor Common

Sopwell •
Nunnery

• Bovingdon

King's Langley

BUCKINGHAMSHIRE

• Abbots Langley

• Sarratt

Radlett

• Aldenha

Cassiobury •

• Watford
Bushey

Els

• Moor Park

| 0 | | 5 | | 10 Miles |
|---|---|---|---|---|

| 0 | 5 | 10 | 15 Kilometres |
|---|---|---|---|

# Ã gazetteer of Gothick places

## Abbots Langley

Abbots Langley was the birthplace in 1615 of one of Britain's most prolific women, Elizabeth Jones. Married to Thomas Greenhill of Hyde Manor in 1631, when she was sixteen, she was pregnant every year thereafter to the age of 54, dying ten years after her last delivery. She was no doubt exhausted: her 38 confinements produced 39 children, all of whom lived to be adults — astonishing in days of high infant mortality.

In the church is a memorial tablet to the only English Pope, Nicholas Breakspear, born near Bedmond. As Adrian IV, he granted special privileges to St Albans. He died in 1159, by poison, according to the chronicle of St Albans Abbey, although the seventeenth-century historian Thomas Fuller claimed that he was choked by a fly.

*OS 166: TL 0903. 3 miles (5 km) north of Watford, signposted off the A41.*

## Albury

In about 1800, one of Albury church's four bells fell to the foot of the tower, whence after a time it vanished. Some say it was stolen by thieves, who were pursued and dropped it into nearby Halls Garden Pond, as deep as the church was high. Others claim it was stolen by the Devil, who hid the bell in the pond because it was bottomless.

*OS 167: TL 4324. Village 3 miles (5 km) east of Puckeridge off the A120 via Albury Road from Little Hadham.*

## Aldbury

The old stocks and their attached whipping-post still stand by Aldbury pond, near to the site of the former ducking-stool used for the chastisement of scolds and 'women of easy virtue'. The stocks were last used as late as 1835 to punish a drunk, and men and women alike would be manacled to the whipping-post and whipped bare-backed for a variety of offences. It may have been against such a post that in 1732 a labourer called Kilby was punished after being sentenced at Hertford to be whipped 'until his back be bloody' for stealing a tobacco box worth 10d.

There was lawlessness of a different order in December 1891, when two Aldbury men were murdered by three Tring poachers. William Puddephatt and Joseph Crawley, second keeper and night watchman on the Stocks

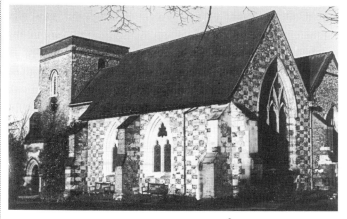

*Abbots Langley church contains a memorial to the only English Pope. The village was the birthplace of one of Britain's most prolific women.*

estate, went out one night to patrol for poachers in the Nowers wood. When they did not return the next morning, the head keeper went to search for them and in a field called Marlins at the edge of the wood he found Crawley's body lying in a pool of blood, his skull crushed and his nose broken. Further on, he discovered Puddephatt with his head battered in.

A known poacher, Walter Smith, who could not give a satisfactory account of his movements on the Saturday night, was taken into custody 'on suspicion' and later two others, Frederick Eggleton and Charles Rayner, were arrested. At their trial they said that the keepers had caught them in the wood and in the ensuing fight the poachers had got the better of their assailants. Walter Smith, claiming that he had fled the fight before the murders were committed, was convicted only of manslaughter and given twenty years' hard labour, but the other two were condemned to death and hanged.

The parish also has its ghosts. The road from Aldbury to Tring is haunted by Simon Harcourt and his phantom coach. They are never seen, but the jingling of harness and the rumbling of wheels can be plainly heard.

*OS 165: SP 9612. Village 3 miles (5 km) north-west of Berkhamsted off the B4506 via Tom's Hill Road.*

# Aldenham

Standing picturesquely by the reservoir, reached from Aldenham by Hilfield Lane, stands what appears to be a medieval castle complete with gatehouse and portcullis. This is Hilfield, built in about 1805 by the architect Sir Jeffry Wyatville as an exercise in 'Gothick' and originally known as Sly's Castle.

*OS 166: TQ 1398. Village 2 miles (4 km) north-east of Watford off the B462 (Hartspring Lane). Hilfield Castle, TQ 154963.*

# Anstey

Behind the parish church and reached through its churchyard lie the overgrown mound and moat of medieval Anstey Castle. From here a secret passage is supposed to run for nearly a mile to Cave Gate in the parish of Wyddial, west of Anstey. Rediscovered in 1904, the apparent cave was perhaps the entrance to a prehistoric flint mine. Tradition maintains that in 1831 an old fiddler known as Blind George undertook to explore the secret passage for a wager. He set out with his dog from Cave Gate, playing as he went, so that the villagers above ground could follow his progress. But suddenly the fiddling ceased, there was a terrible shriek, and then silence. The villagers rushed back to Cave Gate to see the terrified dog emerge tailless with all its hair singed off. Blind George himself was seen no more and since then no

*Both men and women have been manacled to whipping-posts like this at Aldbury, which forms part of the village stocks, last used in 1835.*

*The overgrown moat of Anstey Castle, supposed terminus of a secret tunnel into which Blind George disappeared forever.*

one has dared go into the tunnel, though locals say that its route can be seen in winter because the snow melts first along its course.

*OS 166: TL 4033. Village 4 miles (6 km) north-east of Buntingford off the A10 via Wyddial Road. Cave Gate, TL 388327, on the left of the road coming from Wyddial, where it meets the B1368. The site of the cave has now been grassed over. Anstey Castle, TL 404330.*

# Ashwell

Graffiti in the parish church of St Mary the Virgin are vivid testimony to past tragedy. On the north wall of the tower, about 5 feet from the floor and cut into the stone, is a sketch of Old St Paul's Cathedral, burned down in the Great Fire of London of 1666. A Latin inscription above it gives a contemporary account of the onset of the Black Death which begins 'The beginning of the plague was in June in the year 1300'. 3 feet below this, three lines of Latin verse record the plague of 1349 and the great wind on St Maur's Day (15th January) a decade later: '1350: wretched, wild and driven

to violence the people remaining became witness at last of a tempest. On St Maur's day this year 1361 it thunders on the earth.'

*OS 153: TL 2639. Village 4 miles (6 km) north-east of Baldock off the A1 via Hinxworth Road/New Inn Road into Hinxworth, then Ashwell Road/Hinxworth Road into Ashwell.*

# Ayot St Lawrence

The eighteenth-century passion for the 'Gothick' has left its mark on Ayot St Lawrence, whose church, designed by Nicholas Revett in 1778, was built because Sir Lionel Lyde thought that the old church of St Lawrence would make a romantic ruin. Not far from the manor house, just beyond Brimstone Wood, a clump of trees reputedly marks the spot where a witch was burnt. It is said to be haunted.

*OS 166: TL 1916. Village 2 miles (4 km) west of Welwyn, from roundabout at north end of High Street, via Kimpton Road and Lord Mead Lane. Brimstone Wood, TL 199174.*

# Baldock

Mournful monuments in St Mary's Church include a rare brass of about 1480 in the north chapel, depicting a couple in their burial shrouds. In the chancel a mural tablet by E. H. Baily shows the deathbed scene of Georgiana Caldecott, who died in 1846 at the age of 21. She lies on a couch with a young woman mourning at her side, and an angel bearing her soul to Heaven.

*OS 166: TL 2433. 6 miles (10 km) west of Stevenage via the B197 and the A6141.*

# Barley

Facing the sign of The Fox and Hounds, which stretches across Church End, is a timber-framed 'cage' or lock-up dating from the seventeenth century. Here drunks would have been left to cool their heels by the parish constable, and minor offenders confined until they could be taken to the appropriate magistrates' court.

*OS 154: TL 3938. Village 3 miles (5 km) south-east of Royston on the B1039. Lock-up, TL 399383.*

# Benington Lordship

On the castle mound of Benington Lordship the ruins of a keep destroyed by King John's henchmen in 1212 were given a new lease of life in 1832 by a landscape gardener, Pulham of Broxbourne. He incorporated the old flint walls with their stone dressings into a mock-Norman gatehouse (with portcullis), which can still be seen.

*OS 166: TL 2923. Village 4 miles (6 km) east of Stevenage via the A602 (Broadhall Way), Broadwater Lane and Benington Road. Open to the public.*

# Berkhamsted

St Paul is said once to have visited Berkhamsted and driven out its snakes

and thunderstorms forever. This may be a memory of an original double dedication of the parish church to both St Peter and St Paul. In popular belief, it was the business of the patron saint of a parish to protect it from evil and natural disasters.

The Great St Hugh, twelfth-century Bishop of Lincoln, once came to Berkhamsted to stop people honouring the spirits at St John's Well. It had long been a pagan well and people would dance round it in the moonlight dressing the well with garlands of flowers, until a Berkhamsted monk dreamed that the waters must be re-dedicated to St John the Evangelist. A shrine was built, with a hospice for pilgrims, and a community of monks set up, in line with Church policy as laid down by Pope Gregory the Great, of christianising sacred pagan sites. Yet although the guardian of the well may have changed, the old practices lingered on. The waters of the well were long believed to cure leprosy, the 'King's Evil' (scrofula) and, as with

*King John's supporters destroyed the castle keep at Benington Lordship in 1212. This gatehouse was built from the remains in the nineteenth century.*

9

many holy wells, afflictions of the eye. In 1400 some washerwomen were prosecuted for doing their washing in the well in the belief that clothes washed in its waters bestowed health on the wearer.

The Civil War left its mark on Berkhamsted, as on other places. Local people say that it was from high ground at Wigginton that Cromwell destroyed Berkhamsted Castle with his cannon, and that in the lane known as Soldiers' Bottom, just before twilight, a detachment of his Roundheads can still be seen, their helmets and pikes glittering in the setting sun.

Another Parliamentarian, Daniel Axtel, lived in Berkhamsted Place, at the top of Castle Hill, built of stone taken from Berkhamsted Castle in the reign of Elizabeth I. A colonel in Cromwell's army, Axtel was the officer in charge of security in Westminster Hall during the trial of Charles I, the castle's previous owner. On the morning of the king's last day — 30th January 1649 — an argument broke out in a small Whitehall room when at the last moment one of the three army officers responsible for carrying out the death warrant, Colonel Hercules Hunks, refused to sign the order of execution. As Cromwell raged at him for being 'a froward, peevish fellow', Axtel appeared in the doorway and said, 'Colonel Hunks, I am ashamed of you; the ship is now coming in to harbour and will you strike sail before we come to anchor?' After the Restoration of Charles II, Axtel reaped his reward by being executed at Tyburn and having his head stuck up at Westminster Hall. A fragment of his home's flint and stone chequer front survives near the house called Ash, as does the ruin of a flint and stone gateway.

*OS 165: SP 9907. 25 miles (40 km) north-west of London on the A41.*

*Bourne Gutter is reputed to flow only in times of war. Just in case, this culvert has been built to let it pass under the A41 at Bourne End near Hemel Hempstead.*

# Bishop's Stortford

Bishop's Stortford has sadly lost its three most colourful inns. The Reindeer, at the corner of High Street and Market Square, was kept as a brothel in 1667 by Mrs Elizabeth Aynsworth, who had already been expelled from Cambridge by the university authorities as a procuress. In Bishop's Stortford, undisturbed, she made a modest fortune. Said the diarist Samuel Pepys: '(A)ll the good fellow(s) of the county come hither.' Gone, too, is The Grapes, whose licensee was hanged in 1903 for murdering his three wives. However, the least savoury, from the customer's point of view, was The Dog's Head in the Pot. Inns of this name generally had a signboard that showed a dog licking out a cooking pot, thought to be a mocking insinuation that the landlady was a slut.

*OS 167: TL 4821. 8 miles (13 km) north of Harlow on the A1184.*

*One of the windows in Bovingdon church was dedicated to St Uncumber. Women used to seek her help to rid themselves of an unwanted husband.*

# Bourne End

Joining the Bulbourne at Bourne End is one of Hertfordshire's 'woe-waters' or intermittent streams held to be prophetic of disaster. This is the Bourne Gutter, believed to appear only 'in times of war or rumours of war'. It flows from near Bottom Farm, at the top of Berkhamsted's Swing Gate Lane, through Bourne End, under the London Road by a culvert near a motel and thence into the Bulbourne.

*OS 166: TL 0206. Village at west end of Hemel Hempstead on the A41 between Hemel Hempstead and Berkhamsted. Part of the Bourne Gutter is marked on OS Pathfinder sheet TL 00/10, between TL 006061 and TL 015057. The best place to see it is right in front of the motel (TL 024064).*

# Bovingdon

One of the five lights in the old church of St Lawrence was dedicated to St Uncumber, the saint officially known as St Wilgefortis. On the Continent also called Liberada or Ont-commene, because she gave people easy deaths and freed them from care, in England she became Uncumber and was sought especially by women who wanted to 'uncumber' themselves of their husbands. One of her main shrines was at Old St Paul's Cathedral, where up to the Reformation matrons would offer her oats: 'If ye cannot slepe, but slumber, Geve Otes unto Saynt Uncumber.'

*OS 166: TL 0103. Village 3 miles (5 km) south-west of Hemel Hempstead via the A41, then the B4505/Box Lane/ Hempstead Road.*

# Boxmoor Common

At the western end of Boxmoor Common, visible from the A41, a small white stone by a group of five chestnut trees marks the grave of Robert Snooks, the last highwayman to be hanged in England, on 11th March 1802. He had robbed the mail in 1800 and two years later was caught and condemned to death. On the cart, with the rope round his neck, he offered his gold watch to anyone who would give him proper burial in a coffin, but no one came forward. The hangman accordingly stripped his corpse, sandwiched him in a truss of straw and buried him under the gallows according to custom. But the

*The grave of Robert Snooks, the last highwayman to be hanged in England.*

Cottage on the left, you will see a gate in the iron railings and a footpath sign. Do not follow the sign. The grave is more or less straight ahead, about 50 yards (46 metres) from the road, immediately left of the chestnut trees.

# Bramfield

Between Bramfield and Bull's Green, along Back Lane, a bridleway from Bramfield to Datchworth, is a deep former chalkpit among woods known as Sally Rainbow's Dell. Sally Rainbow was a local witch who lived in one of the caves in the chalk and was greatly feared by the neighbouring farmers, afraid of having their cattle 'overlooked'. Consequently her Dell was avoided, a situation of which the highwayman Dick Turpin took full advantage. After robbing a coach, he would often hide there knowing that Sally Rainbow's reputation would protect him.

*OS 166: TL 2915. Village 3 miles (5 km) north-west of Hertford via the A602, then Bramfield Road. Sally Rainbow's Dell, TL 293164. Both Back Lane and Sally Rainbow's Dell are clearly marked in the 'OS Hertfordshire Street Atlas' (1986).*

# Braughing

In the sixteenth century Matthew Wall, a farmer of Braughing, was being taken along Fleece Lane to the churchyard for burial when his coffin was dropped. As a result of the jolt he awoke from a state of suspended animation and banged vigorously on the lid to attract the attention of his pall-bearers. They let him out and he lived on for a number of years. His will expressed his gratitude by endowing doles to be distributed to poor but 'virtuous' children and aged parishioners, and providing for the ringing of the church bells every year on 2nd October, the anniversary of his escape. On 'Old Man's Day', as it came to be known, the bells were first muffled and tolled as if for a funeral, and then

next day the spectators had a change of heart and got up a subscription for a coffin. The headstone (and even smaller footstone, not visible from the road) were added in 1904. Local schoolboys used to believe that, if one ran round the grave three times and three times shouted 'Snooks!', he would pop his head up.

*OS 166: TL 0406. South-west district of Hemel Hempstead. The grave is at the western end of Boxmoor Common. From Hemel Hempstead, take the A41 towards Berkhamsted, past the station and under the bridge. Opposite Moor End Farm*

*The stocks beside the gate of the church at Brent Pelham.*

*The romantic image of the highwayman, like Dick Turpin, who used to hide at Sally Rainbow's Dell, Bramfield.*

rung in a wedding peal to commemorate his deliverance.

*OS 166: TL 3925. Village about 1 mile (2 km) north of Puckeridge on the B1368.*

## Brent Pelham

Set in the north wall of the nave of St Mary's Church is a tomb purporting to be that of 'Piers Shonks who died anno 1086'. The story goes that he was a lord of the manor who killed a dragon, only for the Devil to appear, bent on vengeance. He vowed to have Shonks body and soul, whether buried inside the church or out, but Shonks outwitted him by having himself interred 'neither within nor without', but in the wall of the nave. On the tomb you can see an angel bearing his soul to Heaven and what some say is his spear thrust into the dragon's jaws. On the wall behind, a sixteenth-century inscription in Latin and English triumphantly concludes:

Shonke one serpent kills, to'ther defies,
And in this wall as in a fortress lies.

*OS 167: TL 4330. Village 5 miles (8 km) east of Buntingford via the B1038. Note also the fine stocks beside the church gate.*

13

*Clibbon's Post, Bull's Green.*

*OS 166: TL 2717. Hamlet 3 miles (4 km) east of Welwyn via the B1000 (Hertford Road), New Road, Harmer Green Lane and Burnham Green Road. Babb's Green, TL 3915; Queen Hoo Hall, TL 278162. Clibbon's Post is about ⅓ of a mile (0.5 km) along on the right-hand side of the road from Bull's Green to Bramfield (TL 2915).*

# Bull's Green

An abrupt end befell Walter Clibbon or Clibborn, on Saturday 28th December 1782. A piemaker turned footpad living at Babb's Green, near Ware, he and his two sons went out to a wood in Oakenvalley Bottom, near Bull's Green, to rob farmers coming home from Hertford market. The first they stopped was the nephew of Benjamin Whittenbury of Queen Hoo Hall, who afterwards went straight to his uncle. Benjamin took up his stick, called his dog and, with his son and his man, went to investigate. Mistaking them for farmers, the footpads set on them and in the fight that followed the elder Clibbon was shot. The coroner ordered him to be buried where he fell. A stake was erected there as a marker, but the notion has sprung up that it was driven through Clibbon to prevent his corpse walking. Clibbon's Post, as it is called, has been renewed from time to time and still stands there as a memorial.

# Burnham Green

What atrocity lies behind the haunting of White Horse Lane, on the parish boundary between Datchworth and Welwyn, by a headless white horse? He can be heard at night galloping down the lane from Burnham Green, ridden, some say, by the ghosts of the dead. He can also be seen in broad daylight, on the sign of the White Horse public house at the edge of the Green.

*OS 166: TL 2616. 2 miles (4 km) east of Welwyn and the B1000 (Hertford Road) via New Road/Harmer Green Lane.*

# Bushey

In the vestry of St James's Church lies buried Silas Titus (died 1667), the man who planned the escape of Charles I from Carisbrooke Castle and was the reputed author of the notorious pamphlet 'Killing Noe Murder', aimed at procuring the assassination of Cromwell. Born at Bushey in 1612, he is also said to have been the one who at the Restoration suggested the digging up and hanging of Cromwell's corpse and those of other regicides. Cromwell was duly dug up from his grave in Westminster Abbey (a burial place he had denied the king) and on 30th January 1661 hung all day on the gallows at Tyburn. At sunset his body was taken down and buried in the common pit at the foot of the gibbet, while his head was cut off and exposed on Westminster Hall.

OS 166: TQ 1395. 3 miles (4 km) south-
east of Watford on the A411. St James's is
in a widening of the High Street.

# Cassiobury

Near Watford is Cassiobury, home
of the Earls of Essex for more than 250
years. On a charge of being involved
in the **Rye House** Plot in 1683 the first
Earl was arrested at Cassiobury and
committed to the Tower, where he
was later found dead in his cell with
his throat cut. Was it suicide, as the
official record says, or was it, as the
common folk insisted, murder? By
whosoever's hand he died, each year
on 13th July, the anniversary of his
death, his ghost returns to Cassiobury
(now a public park, the house having
been demolished in 1927).

Another ghost, to be encountered at
nearby Ironbridge Lock on the Grand
Union Canal where it passes through
Cassiobury Park, is that of Jack o'
Cassiobury. He was the negro slave of
a wealthy woman whose lands skirted

*The ghostly horse that haunts the parish
boundary at Burnham Green.*

*Prudent bargees shun the waters of Ironbridge Lock in Cassiobury Park for fear of the ghost
of Jack o' Cassiobury.*

the canal and who bitterly resented the waterway. She made Jack, who was enormously strong and agile, harass the coal barges coming through Ironbridge Lock until finally a furious bargee knocked him senseless into the lock and left him to drown. It is said that even today narrowboats on the Grand Union shun the lock after dark for fear of Jack o' Cassiobury's ghost.

*OS 176: TQ 0997. North-west of Watford town centre off the A412 (Rickmansworth Road) via Cassiobury Park Avenue.*

# Cheshunt

Cheshunt Great House, ½ mile north-west of the church, and the gift of Henry VIII to Cardinal Wolsey, once had in an upstairs room an indelible bloodstain. No efforts could remove it, but where diligent house-keepers failed fire has succeeded — the house was burnt down in 1965.

A medieval earthwork, still identifiable in places, ran through the parish and was associated with a curious tenure custom. Marked on old maps as the Bank Line and known as the Boundary Bank, it is said once to have formed the boundary between Mercia and Essex. One can follow much of its course by road and footpath, as it runs up through the western part of Theobalds Park, over Beaumont Green, to Nine Acres Wood. It divides the parish into two parts, 'above' and 'below bank'. Well into the twentieth century, in cases of intestacy, all copyhold property on the east side of the Bank Line ('below bank') was subject to 'Borough English' and went to the youngest son, while that on the west side or 'above bank' was subject to the 'Borough French' made almost universal by the Normans, and went to the eldest. Under old English law, 'cradle-land' (land held by Borough English) was deemed the just reward of the youngest son, the 'hearth child', who stayed at home and looked after his parents, one good reason why in fairytales it is usually the youngest and least adventurous son who wins

the hand of the princess or inherits the kingdom. Sadly this antique custom was abolished in 1925.

*OS 166: TL 3502. 14 miles (22 km) north of London on the A10.*

# Codicote

In St Giles's Church in Bury Lane is a medieval woodcarving, perhaps originally a bench end, but now used as part of a bookstand. It shows a fantastical little beast with a lion's tail, a horse's mane, the cloven hooves of a cow or goat, a grinning baboon's face with a mouthful of teeth and large bat's ears. Carved around his neck is a collar and chain, and he is said to represent the Devil in bondage. He is known in the village as the 'Old Dog' and it is said that if you are brave enough to pat him he will bring you good luck. The Old Dog was once lost but tracked down to the lumber room of The Old Curiosity Shop in Drury Lane, London, and restored to the church.

A wooden grave-rail in the churchyard, to the right of the path to the south door, carries this disturbing inscription:

In Memory Of John Gootheridge.
Who Died October 30th 1824,
In The 79th Year Of His Age.
Reburied A Week Later.

John Gootheridge, a farmer of Nup End, was buried in the usual manner but several days later was found lying above ground again, the victim of resurrection men who had been interrupted at their grisly work. He was accordingly buried again the next week.

*OS 166: TL 2118. Village 2 miles (3 km) north-west of Welwyn on the B656.*

# Datchworth Green

Capped with iron and surrounded with railings, the whipping-post on Datchworth Green is last known to have been used on 27th July 1665,

*St Giles's Church, Codicote. (Above) 'Old Dog', the fantastical form of the Devil in bondage in the church and (below) the wooden grave-rail of John Gootheridge, whose body was disinterred by resurrection men.*

IN MEMORY OF. JOHN GOOTHERIDGE.
WHO DIED OCTOBER 30TH 1824. IN THE 79TH YEAR OF HIS AGE.
REBURIED A WEEK LATER.

*The whipping-post on Datchworth Green (left). A phantom horseless cart trundles from the Green down Rectory Lane (right) towards the churchyard.*

when two vagabonds were publicly flogged here. It is only the most tangible reminder of old cruelties. The phantom horseless cart that trundles along Rectory Lane from the Green towards Datchworth churchyard — a manifestation perhaps of the death-coach or ancient Hellwain that carries off the souls of the dead — is by some connected with the alleged death from starvation of four inmates of the poorhouse in the eighteenth century.

*OS 166: TL 2718. Hamlet 3 miles (5 km) north-east of Welwyn via the B197 (Mardley Hill), then Mardleybury Road. Datchworth church (TL 267194) is on Bury Lane.*

# Devil's Dyke

On the outskirts of Wheathamp-stead, on the north-west side of the road from St Albans to Welwyn, is a massive linear earthwork made by deepening a natural valley. It is 1400 feet long, 130 feet wide and originally, on its western side, 40 feet deep. Sir Mortimer Wheeler in the 1930s thought it formed one side of a 100 acre hillfort, which he suggested may have been the tribal capital of the British chieftain Cassivellaunus, attacked by Caesar in 54 BC. Archaeologists today prefer to set this capital at Ravensburgh Castle, the biggest hillfort in eastern England, and to see the Devil's Dyke as part of a discontinuous system of dykes running between Wheathamp-stead and St Albans.

Whatever its historical origin, like the linear earthwork known as Grim's Ditch near Berkhamsted, the Dyke is testimony to the old belief that the Devil (and before him Woden) was the builder of great earthworks. There is a story that one night a man called Marford John, on his way home late from the pub, was crossing the Dyke when he knew that the Devil was behind him. He could see nothing in the pitch dark and in his fright he began cussing and swearing. This put him in Satan's power and suddenly he felt a terrific blow that knocked him to the ground, where he knew nothing more until the bells of St Helen's Church in Wheathampstead woke him in the morning. After that he took care to leave the pub betimes, but was it really for fear of the Devil? What wife would believe such a yarn?

*OS 166: centred on TL 184134. Marked as Belgic Oppidum, but in 'OS Hertfordshire Street Atlas' (1986) as Devil's Dyke. On south-east outskirts of Wheathampstead, reached via the A6129 (Marford Road) and Dyke Lane.*

# Digswell Hill

One of the highwayman Dick Turpin's favourite haunts along the Great North Road was the old holloway of Monk's Walk, leading to what was then Sherrard's Wood from Digswell. At The Red Lion on Digswell Hill until recently customers used to be shown the seat by the fire where he liked to sit.

*OS 166: TL 2213. At north-west end of Welwyn Garden City. The Red Lion is on the B197 (Great North Road) opposite Sherrards Park Wood.*

*The Devil's Dyke may have been the tribal capital attacked by Julius Caesar in 54 BC.*

*The Red Lion at Digswell Hill where some say Dick Turpin had a favourite seat by the fire.*

19

*The grave of Martha Reay or Ray, shot in 1779 'in a fit of frantick, jealous love' by the Reverend Mr Hackman.*

*The tomb with a door to which the corpse has the key, in Essendon churchyard.*

## Elstree

The present church of St Nicholas was built in 1853, replacing an earlier one popularly supposed to have been built from stones brought from Roman Sulloniacae nearby. The old graveyard contains the graves of two murder victims. One was Martha Reay, mistress of the Earl of Sandwich, shot in the head on 7th April 1779, in the Piazza, Covent Garden, as she was leaving the theatre, by the Reverend Mr Hackman, in the words of Boswell, in 'a fit of frantick jealous love'. He turned his pistol on himself immediately afterwards and tried to beat his head in with the butt but was led away covered in blood and hanged twelve days later at Tyburn. The other murdered person is William Weare, for whose grim story see **Radlett.**

*OS 166: TQ 1795. Village 5 miles (8 km) east of Watford on the A411.*

## Essendon

In the churchyard of St Mary the Virgin, roughly west-northwest of the tower, against the fence, is the table-tomb of the Reverend Richard Orme, for 52 years rector of this parish. He was so fearful of being buried alive that when he died in 1843 he left instructions that his tomb was to be built above the ground and fitted with a door with a lock in it. The key, together with a loaf of bread and a bottle of wine, was put with him in the tomb, which remained unsealed to 1881.

*OS 166: TL 2708. Village 3 miles (4 km) east of Hatfield via the A414 (Hertford Road), B1455 and then B158.*

## Folly Arch, Brookmans Park

The turreted and castellated Folly Arch marks the south entrance of

Gobions, a house once lived in by Sir Thomas More and his family. It was pulled down in 1836 by the owner of Brookmans, leaving as its only memorial this sham-medieval gate, erected by Sir Jeremy Sambrooke (died 1754), and possibly designed by James Gibbs in anticipation by some years of Walpole's 'Gothick'.

*OS 166: TL 2404. 2 miles (3 km) north of Potters Bar. Folly Arch is at the south end by Hawkshead Lane.*

## Frithsden

In the nineteenth century there was a pit on Berkhamsted Common known as Rose's Hole after an old man of Frithsden named Rose who dreamed that there was a large chest of gold buried there which could be won by anyone who could raise it without speaking. He and a neighbour set to work and, after digging a deep hole, they exposed the top of a chest. Rose was so excited that he forgot the condition. 'D--n it, Jack, here it is!' he exclaimed. Scarcely had he uttered the words when the chest sank back into the earth and, although they dug frantically, they never saw it again.

*OS 166: TL 0109. Location 2 miles (3 km) north-east of Berkhamsted off Nettleden Road. Berkhamsted Common, OS 165, SP 9911.*

## Great Amwell

In the graveyard of St John the Baptist Church, situated on the slope of a hill, lies Isaac Reed, the Shakespearean editor. When Dr Johnson was writing his *Lives of the Most Eminent English Poets*, he often visited Reed and his curious library in his rooms at Staple Inn, London. Reed died on 5th January 1807 and appropriately lies under the canting inscription:

Read as he may, he must die at last.

*OS 166: TL 3612. Village roughly 1 mile (1.5 km) south-east of Ware on the A1170.*

## Grim's Ditch

Local superstition claims that the earthwork of Grim's Ditch, said by archaeologists to belong to the Iron Age or to the Anglo-Saxon period, was the creation of Sir Guy de Gravade, a notorious wizard (see **Tring**). Appearing on opposite sides of the Bulbourne Valley, in the parishes of Tring and Wigginton and on Berkhamsted Common, it is a ditch about 35 feet across with a bank surviving in several places. Its longest section, running east from Longcroft in Tring, is 1 mile 740 yards long. But its name, in use since at least 1291, tells us it was once believed to be the work of Grim, a nickname for Woden or Odin, god of war and magic. The most powerful of the pagan gods, in Christian times he was replaced as a builder of earthworks by the Devil (see **Devil's Dyke**).

*OS 165: SP 974080, 958089, TL 002089-014090 (two sections), SP 919088, 959088. Linear earthwork west and north-east of Berkhamsted.*

## Gubblecote

Although the death penalty for witchcraft had been abolished in 1735, in 1751 John Butterfield, a publican of Gubblecote, managed to rouse local feeling against an old woman of Long Marston called Ruth Osborne, whom he claimed had bewitched him and his cattle years before when he was a dairyman. As a result, the town criers of Winslow, Leighton Buzzard and Hemel Hempstead gave out that there would be a ducking for witchcraft at Long Marston on 22nd April. Accounts of what happened next are conflicting, but from the deposition of Ruth's husband, John Osborne, the coroner's inquisition and the evidence of witnesses, it seems that the Osbornes fled to Tring workhouse and that on the morning of the 22nd the parish officers locked them in the church as a precaution. However, when a mob

## Gubblecote

A fanciful depiction of the famous Gubblecote witch drowning when John and Ruth Osborne were ducked by a local mob. Below is Astrope Lane where the ducking is supposed to have taken place. The pond was sited in a field corner by the fingerpost but was filled in during the 1960s. Local people would not walk the lane at night for fear of Ruth's ghost.

attacked the workhouse and threatened to fire the whole town, they had to be given up for the public safety. The crowd dragged them from the church, bore them to Butterfield's inn, The Black Horse at Gubblecote, and from there to Wilstone Green, where they were stripped and bundled up in sheets with their hands and feet tied together. In that helpless condition they were 'swum' for witchcraft in a pond known as Wilstone 'Were' or 'Wear'. They were both over seventy ('crazed with age' said Gilbert White), so not surprisingly Ruth was dead by the time they finished and John died soon after. But now came retribution. At the coroner's inquest which followed, some thirty people were found guilty of wilful murder, though in the event only one was hanged. Ruth Osborne had survived being dragged across the pond on the end of a rope, left in her wet sheet for three-quarters of an hour while her husband was ducked, laid down in the middle of the pond and once more left on the bank; but when they dragged her across the pond again Thomas Colley, a chimney sweep, amused the crowd by pushing her face down with his stick. When her sheet came untied and she got her head above water, cried out and grasped the stick, he wrenched it out of her hand and again thrust her under. On finally being taken out, now quite naked, she was seen to be dead. The surgeon who examined her body said she had died partly from suffocation by mud and water, partly from exposure. When Colley's part came out and it was discovered that he had gone round collecting money from appreciative bystanders, he was sentenced at Hertford Assizes to be hanged and hung in chains in the place where the murder was committed. The locals were revolted by the verdict — 'grumbling and muttering that it was a hard case to hang a man for destroying an old wicked woman that had done so much mischief by her witchcraft'. Nevertheless Colley was hanged, not by the pond, because people there protested, but at Gubblecote Cross, and his body was hung in chains on the same gibbet. There it remained for years and doubtless it was this macabre sight that led to tales of his ghost haunting the spot in the form of a great black dog.

It was not the first time mob rule had held sway in Gubblecote. During the Peasants' Revolt in 1381, a bailiff, William Bragg, was killed by the locals and it may be his ghost — a man in a medieval cap — which is said to haunt the thatched house on the corner.

*OS 165: SP 9015. Location 3 miles (4 km) north-west of Tring on Long Marston Road/Lukes Lane. Long Marston, SP 8915. Wilstone Green, SP 9014.*

# Hatfield (Old)

In the parish church of St Etheldreda, in the north or Salisbury Chapel, the curious may admire the pompous monument of the statesman Robert Cecil, first Earl of Salisbury, who died in 1612. Secretary of State to Elizabeth I and Lord Treasurer under James I, he lies in full state dress on a black marble slab supported by four kneeling figures, the Cardinal Virtues: Temperance, Justice, Fortitude and Prudence. Below him, surrounded by the Virtues, lies a skeleton on a straw mat — a reminder, if one were needed, of the vanity of the world. A more moving memorial in the same chapel is the effigy of William Curll by Nicholas Stone (1617), who has shown him as a corpse lying lax on the floor in his shroud.

If the change-ringers are ringing at Hatfield, listen to the bells. They remember the days of wife-swapping and what they say is this:

> Lend me your wife today,
> I'll lend you mine tomorrow.
> No, I'll be like the chimes of Ware,
> I'll neither lend nor borrow.

*OS 166: TL 2308. East of the A1000 (Great North Road).*

23

# Hatfield House

Hatfield House, home of the Cecils, has sheltered some notable eccentrics, one of whom was James, sixth Earl of Salisbury. It was the talk of the county that, when he ran away from Westminster School, his mother sent him back asking for him to be beaten for his own good. He was past seventeen, and it was generally supposed that this was what sent him to 'the bad'. Five generations later, he was still spoken of in the family as the 'Wicked Earl'. Drinking, whoring, keeping low company, living apart from his wife, and not least driving the public stagecoach to and from London made the 'Coachman Earl' a byword, mocked by Hogarth in a cartoon and meriting two lines in Pope's *Dunciad*.

The Grand Staircase at Hatfield, an immensely skilful, if somewhat overblown, piece of Jacobean carving by John Bucke (about 1612), has elaborate newel posts crowned by lions and naked putti. One of the posts is carved with 'trophies' consisting of gardening tools instead of the usual arms and armour, and with the little relief figure of a gardener. This is generally said to be the celebrated John Tradescant the Elder, gardener at Hatfield (on whom see more under **Weston**).

Hatfield House itself came into being as the result of a swap. When James I visited the statesman Robert Cecil at his mansion of Theobalds he was so impressed that he 'suggested' Robert exchange it for his own palace of Hatfield, originally built for the Bishops of Ely. It was in this palace that Mary Tudor and Elizabeth I lived for years in their childhood, virtual prisoners. Robert diplomatically agreed but proceeded to pull most of the gloomy old palace down and build himself a new house from the materials. The hall range of the Bishop's Palace survived, converted in 1628 to stables. On the south-west wall an inscription commemorates the last charger of the Duke of Wellington, a descendant of the famous Copenhagen which he rode at Waterloo.

In Hatfield Park once stood a famous old oak, Queen Elizabeth's Oak, by long tradition supposed to be the tree under which Elizabeth was sitting reading when the news was brought of the death of Queen Mary. The hat she was wearing when she received the message is still preserved in the house. The oak was already little more than a hollow trunk by the end of the nineteenth century. It is said that Queen Victoria took away with her what turned out to be the tree's last acorn for planting at Windsor, since when it has produced no more. The dead trunk is now preserved in the shop in the Stable Yard and Queen Elizabeth II planted a new oak on the spot in 1985.

*OS 166: TL 2308. East of the A1000 (Great North Road) in Old Hatfield. Hatfield House and the Royal Palace of Hatfield both open to the public.*

# Hertford

In Hertford in 1855 the body of a young girl was found with scratches on the shoulders and breasts, and burns on the legs. She was widely supposed to be a victim of the notorious Spring Heeled Jack, whose reign of terror began in the Home Counties in the late 1830s. Described as a leaping, cloaked figure and conjectured to have springs in his heels that enabled him to bound over hedges, he would leap out on travellers at night and attack women and girls. Several murders were laid at his door, but every attempt to catch him failed, possibly because he was more of a bogeyman than a real criminal. Certainly the Hertford murder was not his work — a local man later confessed to having killed the girl when she resisted his advances and having attempted to burn the corpse.

St Andrew's Church in St Andrew's Street replaced an earlier Perpendicular church on this site in 1869. In the old graveyard a headstone commemorates

*All that remains of the old palace at Hatfield, where both Mary Tudor and, later, her sister Elizabeth I were kept as virtual prisoners in their childhood.*

William Hart, who died in 1823, at the age of 66.

> Blow Boreas blow, let Neptune's billows roar
> Here lies a sailor safe landed on the shore;
> Though Neptune's waves have tossed him to and fro
> By God's decree he harbours here below;
> He now at anchor lies amid the fleet
> Awaiting orders Admiral Christ to meet.

*OS 166: TL 3212. 20 miles (32 km) north of London on the river Lea.*

# Hertingfordbury

Among the monuments in St Mary's Church, a fine relief by Roubiliac in the Cowper Chapel shows Spencer Cowper (died 1727), brother of the first Earl Cowper and judge of the Common Pleas, flanked by the figures of Prudence and Justice. Cowper is probably best known for his own trial in 1699, when he was charged with the murder of a Quakeress, Sarah Stout, in whose mother's house he would stay when visiting Hertford. On one occasion after he had been to see them (to break off the connection according to the defence), Miss Stout was found floating among the stakes

of a mill-dam on the Priory River at Bayford. The judge hearing the case was unable to sum up, allegedly because he felt faint and could not recall the evidence. Cowper was not retried but acquitted and guidebooks insinuate that this was a blatant miscarriage of justice. Yet although Cowper's relationship with the lady was dubious, the case was and still is strong for Sarah Stout's death having been suicide. Mud sticks, however, the mud in this case having been thrown by unscrupulous Tories, who stood to gain two seats in Parliament by discrediting Cowper and his influential Whig family.

*OS 166: TL 3012. Location about 1 mile (2 km) west of Hertford on the A414 (Hertingfordbury Road). Bayford, TL 3108.*

# Hinxworth Place

Originally built as a monastery for White Monks (or Cistercians) in the eleventh century, the old house of Hinxworth Place, dating from the fifteenth, has a horrific memorial of the fate said to have met one of its inmates. On the wall alongside one of

25

the small staircases leading to the attic this message is inscribed:

This is where a monk
was buried alive in this wall.
His cries can be heard sometimes
at midnight. 1770.

*OS 153: TL 2339. House 4 miles (7 km) north of Baldock via the A1 and Hinxworth Road.*

# Hitchin

According to the poet George Chapman (*c*.1559-1634), probably born at 35 Tilehouse Street, it was at the command of Homer's ghost, appearing to him on Hitchin Hill, that he translated the *Iliad* and the *Odyssey*.

More than two hundred years later, it was due to another ghost that Hitchin was not the scene of a terrible rail disaster. A retired engine driver reported that once, when he was running late on the Great Northern, the train was passing through Hatfield without stopping when a sad-faced man in black stepped off the platform on to the footplate. When he put his hand on the regulator, the driver felt compelled to place his own hand there too and the touch of that other hand seemed to him 'like the touch of snow'. He found he had cut off the steam and, though the signal showed

a clear line and the fireman, who had not seen the man in black, protested, he stopped the train at Hitchin. It was as well he did — there were two trucks across the line and neither he nor his passengers would have survived the impact had they crashed.

Hitchin's most endearing ghosts may possibly still be heard where, behind the Georgian Sun Inn in Sun Street, a bowling green used to run down to the river Hiz. Here on summer evenings in the eighteenth century Mark Hildesley, the vicar of Hitchin, would play a game of bowls with Edward Young, the rector of **Welwyn.** It is evidently not the usual remorse of ghosts but friendly rivalry that keeps the two clergymen tied to this spot, where in summer you can hear the click of bowls and Young's voice arguing over the score.

Remorse does play a part, perhaps, in another haunting. Hitchin was home for a time of Eugene Aram, the scholar-murderer, who in 1750 was an usher in the Church School, Golden Square. Five years earlier he had murdered the shoemaker Daniel Clark in St Robert's Cave near Knaresborough, North Yorkshire. Clark disappeared in 1745 when he was known to be in possession of valuable goods and some of these were found in Aram's garden. He was arrested and tried, not

*At the Sun Inn, Hitchin, some say that the click of the bowls played in the eighteenth century by the vicars of Welwyn and Hitchin can still be heard.*

for murder, but for conspiring with Clark in a swindle. Acquitted for want of evidence, he embarked on a nomadic life as a schoolmaster. Then a skeleton was found near Knaresborough and an accomplice excited suspicion by protesting too loudly that it was not Clark's. He was driven at last to confess where they had hidden the body, the bones were exhumed and identified, and Aram was suddenly arrested at King's Lynn in Norfolk. He was tried at York on 3rd August 1759 and, despite spiritedly conducting his own defence, was found guilty and hanged three days later. There are macabre accounts of his widow having gathered up his fallen bones from beneath the gibbet on which he hung rotting, and his children pointing out his corpse to strangers for pennies. He was made the subject of a novel by Bulwer Lytton of **Knebworth House** and at the beginning of the twentieth century a narrow passage from the churchyard into High Street was still known as Aram's Alley and thought to be haunted by his ghost.

*OS 166: TL 1829. 8 miles (13 km) north-east of Luton on the A505.*

# Hunsdon

A brass plate in St Dunstan's Church, close by Hunsdon House, commemorates with grim irony the death of James Gray, 'Parke and Hous-keper' at Hunsdon, who died in 1591. Etched on the brass is the hunter hunted — Death as a skeleton stabbing Gray as he takes aim at a stag. Death says, *Sic pergo*, 'So proceed I' (in other words 'I do as you do').

*OS 167: TL 4114. Village 4 miles (6 km) east of Ware via the B1004 to Widford, then south on the B180 (Hunsdon Road).*

# Hyde Hall

Sir John Jocelyn of Hyde Hall near Sawbridgeworth was an eccentric who is said to have quarrelled frequently with the vicar and flatly refused to be buried in the churchyard. Consequently, when he died on 1st November 1741, according to his own instructions he was interred at sunset, with his horse, in the circle of yew trees in the avenue leading to the hall and his best ox was slaughtered to feast the parish poor.

*OS 167: TL 497154. House (on map shown as Great Hyde Hall) 1 mile (2 km) north-east of Sawbridgeworth off Sawbridgeworth Road.*

# Ickleford

From Ickleford comes a sixteenth-century instance of Catch 22 — a man called Harding living here claimed to be a witch, but his charms for curing illness and so forth failed so often that in 1590 he was sent to prison for fraud.

*OS 166: TL 1831. About 1 mile (2 km) north of Hitchin on the A600.*

# King's Langley

In All Saints parish church, the carved and painted tomb-chest of Edmund of Langley, fifth son of Edward III and the first Duke of York, offers a curious sidelight on Tudor foreign policy. In 1366, when Pedro the Cruel of Castile was driven from the throne, he fled with his two daughters, Constance and Isabel, to Bordeaux, which was then English territory. There he enlisted the support of the Black Prince, and through him his father, Edward III. While in Bordeaux, the two girls met Edward's other sons, John of Gaunt and Edmund of Langley. All three brothers took part in an expedition that placed Pedro back on the throne, but two years later he was killed in a mêlée. Constance and Isabel took refuge with the English again and in due course Constance married John and Isabel Edmund. By these marriages, English John became ancestor of the kings of Spain, while from Castilian Isabel descended Edward IV, Edward V,

*The tomb-chest of the first Duke of York is in All Saints Church, King's Langley.*

Richard III and Elizabeth of York (married to Tudor Henry VII to bolster his claim to the throne). With Spain's claim to England in some respects more legitimate than their own, small wonder the Tudors alternately courted and hated the Spanish.

OS 166: TL 0702. *Village 3 miles (4.5 km) south of Hemel Hempstead. Site of Royal Palace, TL 065025.*

# Knebworth House

Knebworth House is a monument to early nineteenth-century ideas of the Gothick or pseudo-medieval and was the home of novelist Bulwer Lytton (Edward George Bulwer-Lytton, first Baron Lytton). The Lyttons had a family death-warning in the form of a Radiant Boy. Among those he visited was Lord Castlereagh, when he was staying in the house some years before his suicide in 1822 when he slit his throat with a penknife. A naked 'burning babe' appeared out of the grate, increasing in size as it approached him, then dwindled into the fire again. Unfortunately the room in which 'Cut-throat Castlereagh' witnessed this apparition was in a part of the house which has been demolished.

Another ghost said to haunt Knebworth is Jenny Spinner, a woman at a spinning wheel. Though some suspect her history began with a tale written by a Miss James at Knebworth one Christmastime around 1800, in 1707 there was a 'Haunted Chamber' and an inventory of 1797 mentions 'Spinning Jenny's Room'. Because this room was also in the part of the house later demolished, Spinning Jenny's ghost is now said to haunt the park and gardens. The daughter of the head gardener there in the middle of the twentieth century says her father often saw the ghost in the kitchen garden.

On a quiet note, near one of the paths in the garden a small memorial was erected by Bulwer Lytton to a favourite dog. It reads:

> Alas! poor Beau.
> (Died Feb. 28, 1852)
> It is but to a Dog that this stone
> is inscribed:
> yet what now is left
> within the home of thy Fathers,
> O Solitary Master,
> that will grieve for thy departure,
> or rejoice at thy return?
> E.B.L.

The monument seems to have set a precedent and was followed by an even more touching one in marble near the rose-garden, originally surmounted by 'a vase of fragrant musk' and bearing the words: 'Here lies the Great heart of A little Dog BUDGET Died 5 June 1886'. Today, behind the yew-hedge in the rose-garden, there is a whole colony of little graves.

*OS 166: TL 2320. House 2 miles (4 km) south of Stevenage off the B197 (London Road) via Old Knebworth Lane. Open to the public.*

# Layston

Reached by way of Church Street, Buntingford, is the ruined church of St Bartholomew. Once it belonged to the deserted medieval village of Layston; then it served Buntingford until the building there of St Peter's at the beginning of the seventeenth century.

In other parts of Britain, when a church is far from the village it serves, this is explained as the result of the Devil having moved it, but St Bartholomew's pleasant hillside site is said to have been chosen for it by fairies. Though Layston village was a ruin by 1700, the bells of St Bartholomew's continued to be heard, especially on dark nights. Once in the nineteenth century the bellringers at Buntingford heard them announcing evensong and went to see who was ringing them. When they got to the church they found it lit, but as soon as they entered the lights went out and the ringing stopped.

*OS 166: TL 3630. About 1 mile (2 km) north-east of Buntingford (north of Ware on the A10) via Church Street. The*

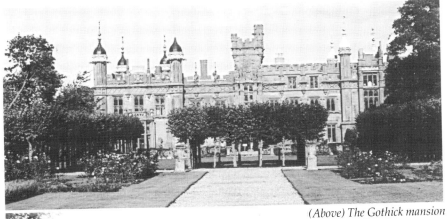

*(Above) The Gothick mansion at Knebworth, where Spinning Jenny haunts the kitchen garden.*

*The bells rang in the church of St Bartholomew, Layston, long after it was abandoned.*

29

fourteenth-century chancel of St Bartholomew's is kept in repair by the Friends of Layston Church and is at times used for services. The Friends are now replacing the roof of the nave.

# Lemsford

Brocket Hall, Lemsford, was the home of the somewhat peculiar Lady Caroline Lamb (1785-1828), wife of William Lamb, Lord Melbourne. Once, when rejected by Lord Byron, she had a huge bonfire lit in the grounds, round which hapless village girls, clad all in white, were compelled to dance. She herself contributed to the proceedings by reciting an elegy which she had composed and ritually burning Byron's portrait.

OS 166: TL 2112. Village about 1 mile (2 km) west of Welwyn Garden City. Brocket Hall, TL 2123, north of the village.

# Little Gaddesden

In an old cottage in Witchcraft Bottom, Little Gaddesden, lived Rosina Massey, wife of the mystic poet Gerald Massey (1828-1907) and commonly thought to be a witch. It was said that a child looked through her window one evening and saw her with hands outstretched conducting the cups and saucers in a dance round the table.

She could likewise make her three-legged stool run errands for her and on windy nights would ride a hurdle from the bottom of her garden across to Studham and back. On 3rd May 1866 she prepared her coffin, which had been in her house some time, and, taking a candle, a penny and a hammer, lay herself down in it to die. The candle was to light her way through the darkness, the penny to pay her toll, and the hammer to knock upon the doors of Heaven. She was buried in the churchyard just inside the gate leading to the vestry.

Little Gaddesden had already had a taste of magic. In 1664 two small imps came riding down a chimney on a stick and so bewitched Mary Hall, the blacksmith's daughter, that she spoke in two voices, neither of them her own.

OS 165: SP 9913. Village 4 miles (6 km) north of Berkhamsted via Nettleden Road. Witchcraft Bottom is reached by the stile and footpath opposite the Bridgewater Arms. Rosina's cottage is said to be one of those constituting 'Faerie Hollow', a private residence. The Bridgewater Arms has interesting old photographs.

# Little Hadham

In the parish church of St Edmund the Martyr, on the south side of the chancel, is a memorial stone to Arthur,

Faerie Hollow, Little Gaddesden, is said to incorporate the cottage where Rosina Massey, whom local people believed to be a witch, used to live.

Lord Capel, executed for his loyalty to King Charles I. A devoted Royalist who fell into Parliamentary hands at the surrender of Colchester (1648), he was sent to the Tower of London, whence he managed to escape, only to be arrested again shortly after. He was tried for treason at Westminster and beheaded in Old Palace Yard on 9th March 1649. Before his execution he expressed a wish for his heart to be buried with the king. The Bishop of Winchester accordingly preserved Capel's heart in a silver box, which at the Restoration he gave to Charles II. The King must have sent it to Lord Capel's son, first Earl of Essex, for in 1703 it was found in the muniment room at Hadham Hall, the family home. It is on record as having been transferred to **Cassiobury** in 1809, but what became of it thereafter is unknown.

*OS 167: TL 4322. Village 3 miles (5 km) west of Bishop's Stortford on the A120 (Stane Street). Hadham Hall, TL 4522, is east of the village.*

## Little Wymondley

A subterranean passage is supposed to run westwards from the cellars of the thirteenth-century priory of Black Canons at Little Wymondley to Delamere House at Great Wymondley, once the home of Cardinal Wolsey. It is said to have been the terror of children at the beginning of the nineteenth century, when it was still open.

*OS 166: TL 2127. Village 3 miles (4 km) south-east of Hitchin on the A602 (Stevenage Road). Of the remains now forming part of The Priory, a farm on Priory Lane, only the moat is visible from the road.*

## Markyate Cell

The beautiful neo-Jacobean mansion of Markyate Cell is lent an added romance by the legend of the Wicked Lady, one of the Ferrers family into whose hands the Cell, a former priory, fell after the Reformation. The Wicked Lady was Lady Katherine Ferrers, said to have lived at Markyate in the eighteenth century and to have led a double life as a highwaywoman. Dressed in men's clothes and a mask, she would creep out at night by a secret stair and on a black horse swift as the wind rob travellers on the Holyhead Road. Her career came to an end when she was shot at **Nomansland** and dragged herself home, to be found lying dead outside the door to the secret stair. This door was subsequently blocked up and the stone stair only revealed again when the house was being rebuilt after a fire in 1840 had destroyed much of it. People generally believed that the fire was the Wicked Lady's work and many of the local men who had come to tackle the blaze swore they had seen Lady Ferrers swinging herself on the branch of a sycamore near the house. She is said still to ride the roads around Markyate at night.

*OS 166: TL 0517. House north of Markyate village 4 miles (6 km) south-west of Luton on the A5.*

## Mimram Valley

The valley of the river Mimram, near Welwyn, was used in the nineteenth century by Jean-François Gravelet, better known as Blondin, to practise his famous stunt of walking the tightrope across the Niagara Falls blindfold, pushing a wheelbarrow, with a man on his back. At the time he was staying with the scientist George Dering at Lockleys House, Welwyn.

*OS 166: TL 2312. The river rises north of Whitwell, flows south-east into the river Lea at Hertford and east of Welwyn runs roughly parallel to the B1000 (Hertford Road).*

## Minsden Chapel

The ghost of a monk haunts the picturesque ruins of Minsden Chapel, once a chapel-of-ease serving nearby Langley and Preston. Built on its hilltop in the fourteenth century, it

Lady Katherine Ferrers, the Wicked Lady who was a highwaywoman, owned Markyate Cell (above) and perhaps still rides the roads of Markyate at night. She was shot at Nomansland (left), where the pub is named after her.

has been ruined from 1650 at least, though weddings were celebrated within its walls until 1814. The monk's appearance, at Hallowe'en, is preceded by the tolling of a lost chapel bell and music is heard. He walks from the crumbling south arch, up steps that are no longer there, and fades away with the music.

*OS 166: TL 198246. Remains 3 miles (5 km) south of Hitchin and reached by bridleway from the Royal Oak pub on the B656 (London Road) or from the B651 to St Paul's Walden.*

## Moor Park

Treason seems to have been in the air of Moor Park, in the parish of Rickmansworth. What you see today is the grand eighteenth-century re-modelling of a seventeenth-century house, now the clubhouse for a golf course. It lies some way south-west of the old Manor of the More, begun about 1426 and thereafter enlarged by

*Here at Minsden Chapel the bell tolls before the ghost of a monk appears.*

a series of owners. First was George Neville, fifteenth-century Archbishop of York and Lord Chancellor of England. When he was convicted of High Treason, it fell forfeit to the Crown and was eventually given by Henry VIII to Cardinal Wolsey. He lived here before moving to Hampton Court, subsequently dying in 1530 on his way to the Tower of London. The second house was lived in for a time by the Duke of Monmouth, son of Charles II and Lucy Walter. He was one of those involved in the **Rye House** Plot (1683). After the failure of the Monmouth Rebellion and his defeat at Sedgemoor (6th July 1685), he was dragged from a Somerset ditch to be executed on 15th

*Moor Park, home of George Neville and, later, the Duke of Monmouth, both executed for High Treason.*

July on Tower Hill. The executioner, the famous Jack Ketch, failed to kill the duke with the axe and his head finally had to be severed with a knife.

*OS 176: TQ 0793. House 1 mile (2 km) south-east of Rickmansworth between the A4145 (Moor Lane) and A404 (London Road). Open to the public.*

# Nomansland

Nomansland is a large tract of common stretching west from the road between Sandridge and Wheathampstead. Like other pieces of land bearing this name, it is said to be forbidden ground, because of an old superstition that one piece of land in every parish had to be left uncultivated as a tribute to the Devil, or else he would wither the crops. In fact it lies between the former lands of the abbeys of St Albans and Westminster.

A freehouse called The Wicked Lady stands at the corner where Dyke Lane leads up to the **Devil's Dyke** (signposted). The sign shows a highwaywoman — for her story see **Markyate Cell.**

*OS 166: TL 1712. Common 1 mile (2 km) south of Wheathampstead, west of the B651.*

# Northchurch

On the south wall in St Mary's Church is a brass tablet inscribed to

'Peter the Wild Boy', found in the forest of Hertswold near Hanover in 1725. Black-haired and naked, apparently about twelve years old, he had been living on berries and nuts, and in repose would drop on to all fours like an animal. Word of him reached George I, Britain's first Hanoverian king, and to please the then Princess of Wales, Caroline of Ansbach, Peter was brought to England. At first he was kept at Court, but all efforts to teach him to speak having failed (though he liked music), the Court lost interest and Peter was literally farmed out in Hertfordshire, first at Haxter End, and later at Broadway. Living at Haxter End in the care of a farmer named James Fenn, on an allowance of £35 *per annum*, Peter proved still a rover, once wandering as far as Norwich and ending up in the Bridewell. After this, Fenn had a leather collar made for him which bore the message: 'Peter the wild man from Hanover. Whoever will bring him to Mr Fenn, at *Berkhamsted*, Hertfordshire, shall be paid for their trouble.' When he died on 22nd February 1785, Peter was believed to be in his early seventies. His gravestone is in the churchyard, just opposite the porch.

*OS 165: SP 9708. North-west district of Berkhamsted on the A41. The brass tablet carries a likeness of Peter engraved by W. Cole. Peter's collar still exists, in the keeping of Berkhamsted School for Boys.*

# Piccotts End

Number 140 Piccotts End, one of a cluster of cottages on the boundary of Hemel Hempstead Old Town, is thought to have been built as a hospice for pilgrims on their way to venerate the relic of the Holy Blood at Ashridge. In 1826 it became the first cottage hospital in England. Inside, late medieval wall paintings of religious subjects include St Catherine of Alexandria, martyred by being torn to death between spiked wheels (the origin of the 'catherine wheel' firework), and mysterious symbols which express the Catharist heresy of the Albigensians in southern France. Essentially the Cathars believed that the material world was created by the Devil. Many took this to mean that they were Devil worshippers and the hideous persecution of the Albigensians by the Inquisition in the thirteenth century set the pattern for the subsequent witchcraft trials. Ironically, the paintings now vie for attention with a priest's hiding place in the roof, designed to shelter Catholic priests from *their* persecutors after the Reformation.

*OS 166: TL 0509. At the north end of Hemel Hempstead, via High Street/Piccotts End road. Number 140 also has a medieval well and a collection of religious artefacts and memorabilia.*

*The grave of Peter the Wild Boy at Northchurch.*

I and founded the church. This and the water-filled moat seem to have inspired the wishful rhyme:

In Pirton Pond
There lies untold
Sacks of treasure,
Pots of gold.

*OS 166: TL 1431. Village 3 miles (5 km) north-west of Hitchin on the B655 (Pirton Road). Coming from Hitchin, turn right up Walnut Tree Road and continue round to the church. The motte is reached by a path through the churchyard.*

(Above) The first cottage hospital in England houses remarkable wall paintings with Catharist symbols.

Pirton motte beside Pirton pond, supposed to be filled with treasure.

# Rableyheath

West of the village is Sally Deards Lane, linking Rabley Heath Road and Bury Lane (both of them leading into Codicote). Sally Deards was a witch of Rableyheath who could turn herself into a hare and was eventually shot as such by a gamekeeper. Hares have

# Pirton

St Mary's Church at Pirton stands within the oval bailey of a motte-and-bailey castle. The motte, locally known as Toot Hill and still partly moated, is just outside the churchyard to the south-west. Some believe it to be pre-Norman and its popular name suggests that, like other 'toothills', it served as a look-out. Whether it did or not, a castle is generally thought to have been built here by Ralph de Limesy, who received the manor from William

long been associated with magic — Boudicca carried a hare into battle with her and released it to strike fear among the Romans. That witches could turn themselves into hares to escape pursuit, and bear on their bodies wounds inflicted on them as wer-animals was widely believed. In Hertfordshire witches and hares are still connected in superstition. An old saying goes, if you see a hare run downhill, expect a fire.

*OS 166: TL 2319. Hamlet 2 miles (3 km) north of Welwyn, via the B197 (Great*

35

*North Road), Canonsfield Road and Potters-field Road.*

# Radlett

In 1823 Gills Hill Lane, near Batlers Green, Radlett, was the scene of the notorious Gills Hill Murder or 'Hertfordshire Tragedy'. Boxer and gamekeeper John Thurtell murdered a solicitor, William Weare, for having cheated him at billiards. Weare accepted an invitation to spend the weekend with Thurtell's associate William Probert in Gills Hill Lane, and travelled down from London with Thurtell in a gig. Arriving at Radlett, Thurtell shot him point blank and cut his throat, and Probert and James Hunt (another boon companion) helped dump the corpse in a pond. But some Radlett labourers found the pistol and knife, Probert turned King's Evidence and his erstwhile cronies were condemned to death. Hunt's sentence was commuted to transportation, but Thurtell himself was hanged in front of Hertford Gaol. Probert, too, ended on the gallows the following year, not for murder, but horse-stealing.

*OS 166: TL 1699. 5 miles (8 km) south of St Albans on the A5183 (Watling Street). Gills Hill Lane runs off the B462 (Watford Road). It continues down into Loom Lane, running to Batlers Green (TL 1598) at the south end of Radlett.*

# Redbourn

Although in the Middle Ages a great many barrows or tumuli were ransacked by treasure hunters, sometimes under licence from the Crown, it was the desire for relics that in 1178 led the monks of **St Albans** to open the long-since destroyed 'Hills of the Banners' at Redbourn. They were looking for the remains of St Amphibalus, who according to legend was a priest whom Alban sheltered from persecution and by whom he was converted. Amphibalus was eventually captured in Wales and put to death at Redbourn. Although the Hills of the Banners

were probably Anglo-Saxon barrows and even the saint's existence is in doubt (his name a translator's misunderstanding of the Latin for 'cloak'), at the time the monks were satisfied that what they had found was indeed Amphibalus. The relics gave a satisfactory boost to his cult, attracting pilgrims to his shrine until it was destroyed at the Reformation.

*OS 166: TL 1012. Village 4 miles (7 km) north-west of St Albans on the A5183 (Watling Street). The base of St Amphibalus's shrine remains in St Albans Abbey.*

# Royston

In Royston town centre, reached by a tunnel from Melbourn Street, is Royston Cave, the subject of much speculation. Nearly 30 feet deep and bottle-shaped, it was discovered accidentally in 1742. Crudely carved reliefs of the Crucifixion, St Christopher and other subjects covered the walls, Christian and pagan symbols mingling together, and many suggestions have been made as to their origin — some attribute them to the Knights Templar. The likeliest theory seems to be that it was a Roman or Saxon dene-hole or chalk pit subsequently used as a hermitage and then sealed up by the lord of the manor in the reign of Henry VIII.

*OS 154: TL 3540. 12 miles (20 km) south-west of Cambridge, at crossing of Icknield Way and Ermine Street (A505 and A14/A10). Royston Cave, TL 360408. Open to the public on Saturdays, except in winter.*

# Rye House

The Rye House, at the north-east end of Hoddesdon, is famous for the Rye House Plot, a conspiracy to waylay and murder Charles II and James, Duke of York, as they returned from Newmarket races. All that remains of it is the gatehouse, on a moated site beside the river Lea, but in the days of Charles II it was the home of Richard Rumbold, a former officer in the

Parliamentary army. He and other malcontents hatched a plot in the spring of 1683 to intercept Charles and his brother on their way back to London by placing an overturned cart in the road and shooting them in the confusion. However, the royal party returned sooner than expected, the plot leaked out and the Rye House was searched. A number of noble persons were accused of conspiracy, including the Earl of Essex (see **Cassiobury**) and the Duke of Monmouth (see **Moor Park**). Rumbold himself is said to have been hanged near the Rye House.

*OS 166: TL 385100. Moated site and gatehouse 1 mile (2 km) from the centre of Hoddesdon via Rye Road, north-east of the Rye House Inn.*

# St Albans

St Albans owes its name to the first British martyr, Alban, a citizen of the Roman town of Verulamium, who was put to death by the Romans in AD 209 for having sheltered a Christian priest.

A Roman shrine on the site of his execution had been replaced by a monastic church by the end of the fourth century, but the 'official' story later put on record by the monks of St Albans was that Offa of Mercia (died 796) was commanded in a vision to search for the body of St Alban and build a monastery on the spot. He came to Verulamium and found Alban's relics on a wooded height known as Holmhurst. There he built a church and founded a Benedictine monastery.

When in the early eleventh century Ealdred, the eighth abbot of St Albans, began to rebuild the abbey, he gathered the stones for the work from the ruins of Roman Verulamium. In the course of this destruction, he came upon a site apparently famous as having been the lair of a dragon — a cavern and ravine known as Wermenhert (in Old English a dragon was *wyrm*, or 'worm'). This he 'flattened as far as he was able', destroying every trace of where the monster had lurked, very likely to quash any pagan superstitions among his parishioners.

A chronicler in the reign of Richard

*The shot which killed William Weare in Gills Hill Lane, Batlers Green, Radlett.*

II says that at the bottom of Holywell Hill on which the abbey stands was a spring believed to have healed the wounds of Uther Pendragon, father of King Arthur, who had fought a great battle against the Saxons here.

The most bizarre episode in the annals of St Albans is probably the protracted skulduggery over St Alban's relics. During the Viking raids of the ninth and tenth centuries, the bones of Alban were stolen and taken to Odense in Denmark (where the cathedral is dedicated to him). The abbot of St Albans sent two monks to Denmark in disguise to steal back the bones and this they claimed they did. The Danes, however, said the purloined bones were not the real ones. Round two began when the relics were sent from St Albans to Ely (then an island) for safety when more Vikings were expected. After their return to St Albans, the monks of Ely claimed that this time *they* had kept the real ones. The abbot of St Albans retaliated by saying that the real ones had not gone to Ely in the first place but been hidden in a wall, the others being a decoy. So who had the fakes and who had the real relics — Odense, Ely or St Albans? Pope Adrian IV (Nicholas Breakspear) said it was St Albans. Naturally — he was a Hertfordshire man.

Among the abbey's other 'relics' were the remains of the 'Good Duke

Humphrey' of Gloucester, brother of Henry V. He was buried there in 1447, in a vault in the chancel accidentally rediscovered in 1703. Daniel Defoe said in 1724 that when the tomb was opened the body was undecayed, but by the mid nineteenth century the strong pickle in which it had been preserved had all dried up and the flesh was wasted. Called the Good Duke because he was a patron of poets and writers, gave the first books for a library at Oxford and was a benefactor of St Albans Abbey, 'good' in other respects he was not. He laid claim to the regency during the minority of Henry VI and when it went to his elder brother, the Duke of Bedford, he made Bedford's life a trial with his greed and political squabbling. Eventually losing influence with the king, in 1441 he found himself unable to prevent witchcraft proceedings against his wife and in 1447 he was placed in custody for High Treason on suspicion of plotting against the king's life. Five days later he was found dead in his bed. Popular suspicions of foul play, say historians, are groundless.

Another royal duke was among the dead at the First Battle of St Albans on 22nd May 1455, the first battle of the Wars of the Roses. This was Edmund, Duke of Somerset, whose body was found on the steps of the Castle Inn, which stood on the corner of Victoria

*According to Shakespeare, Edmund Beaufort had been warned to 'shun castles'.*

*Church Cottages, Sarratt. In this village lived Rebecca, Mary and Anne Baldwin, sisters who were possessed by devils.*

Street. According to Shakespeare's *Henry VI Part 2,* he had received the warning from a spirit conjured up by Mother Jourdain, a witch: 'Let him shun castles.'

St Albans had its own witches, the most famous of whom was Mother Haggy. Wife of a St Albans yeoman in the reign of James I, she only latterly took to black witchcraft. Even after her death she continued to terrorise the neighbourhood with her tricks, which included careering round the town in broad daylight on her broomstick and crossing the Ver on a kettle-drum.

In 1819 the Chester and Holyhead mails, having a race that had begun at Highgate in London, crashed as they were approaching St Albans late at night, the Chester mail deliberately cutting across the other's track and overturning it, killing one of the passengers. The drivers were indicted for murder and convicted of manslaughter, each being sentenced to a year's imprisonment.

*OS 166: TL 1407. 19 miles (31 km) north-west of London on the A5183 (Watling Street).*

# St Ippollitts

In medieval times knights and travellers are said to have brought their horses into the church of St Ippolyts to be blessed: in his lifetime the saint had been a great curer of horses. But is a more ancient folk memory hidden here? Hippolytus, beloved by the goddess Diana, was dragged to his death in the sea by the horses pulling his chariot. Was there an ancient pagan association with Diana and Hippolytus, even a sacred grove, where the church now stands? Historian Margaret Hole asks also whether the ghostly coach and horses said to rush down Lannock Hill in **Weston**, 4½ miles away, are part of the same mystery. They appear at midnight on 12th August, the eve of Diana's own day, 13th August.

*OS 166: TL 1927. 1½ miles (2.5 km) south-east of Hitchin off the B656 from Hitchin to Welwyn.*

# Sarratt

In the early eighteenth century, the Baldwin family of Sarratt were much troubled by possession by 'devils'. John and Rebecca Baldwin had four daughters, of whom three, all between twelve and sixteen, had sporadic bouts of insanity and delusions. In 1700 one of them, Rebecca, began to make noises like a bee, a cat and a dog, and she kept crying out 'I'll burn ye!' and attempting to throw herself on the fire. She grew worse and worse, then in 1702 her youngest sister Mary was seized with fits of dumbness and blindness. They both began to see 'appearances' invisible to others and could only walk backwards, at intervals crying out, 'Now we shall fall down', which they duly did. Later the other sister, Anne, also succumbed. Their father and his friends held prayer meetings at the house until the children were cured. A witness present at Mary's cure reported that she went out of the room in order to vomit 'and cast up (as she thought) a piece of flesh as big as a mouse...and she said she thought the piece of flesh crawled away, and the appearances went away with it snivelling and crying'.

*OS 176: TQ 0499. Village 3 miles (5 km) north of Rickmansworth via A404 (Chorley-wood Road), Solesbridge Lane and Sarratt Road.*

# Shenley

In the churchyard of St Botolph's Church is a wooden grave-rail commemorating Joseph Rogers, who died on 17th August 1828, at the age of 77, having been parish clerk for half a century. On the reverse we read:

Silent in dust lies mouldring here
A parish Clerk of Voice most clear;
None Joseph Rogers could excel
In laying bricks or singing well.
Though snapp'd his line laid by his rod,
We build for him our hopes in God
The Saviour God, that He will raise
Again that Voice to sing His praise
In Temple Blest, Which always stands,
The church of God not made with hands.

*OS 166: TL 1900. Village 5 miles (8 km) south-east of St Albans on the B5378 (London Road). Note also the lock-up or 'cage' in centre of village.*

# Six Hills Barrows

Standing beside the Roman road that underlies the old Great North Road (A1) are six barrows traditionally known as the Six Hills. About 10 feet high and grass-covered, looking like green pudding basins upside down, they are thought to be Roman, but popular tradition says they are the work of the Devil. Coming to Whomerley Wood one night, he dug seven large holes with the intention of throwing the soil at Stevenage. But the earth fell short, creating the Six Hills, while the seventh spadeful knocked the spire off Graveley church and formed a small hill just outside the churchyard. In Whomerley Wood itself, a wilderness between Bedwell and Shephall, the seven holes are supposed still to be visible. Not inappropriately, it is the haunt of a phantom hound.

*OS 166: TL 238236. Tumuli south of Stevenage town centre and north of the College of Further Education, on the south side of Six Hills Way (running east off the A602) in front of Six Hills House (STC). Graveley, TL 2327.*

# South Mimms Castle

In Mymmshall Wood is the tangled and overgrown motte-and-bailey of South Mimms Castle, built by Geoffrey de Mandeville around 1140-2. Tradition says that the castle, already in ruins by the sixteenth century, in its heyday had gates so huge that their shutting could be heard as far off as Winchmore Hill.

It was the stronghold of the wicked Sir Geoffrey, who, being hunted down for one of his crimes, hid from his pursuers in a hollow tree. His hour had come, however, for the tree sank into the castle well and he perished. His ghost, clad in full armour, still haunts the castle mound.

*Six Hills Barrows, traditionally believed to have been six spadefuls of earth dug by the Devil.*

This is no stranger than what Tudor tradition claimed happened to the real Sir Geoffrey, an unscrupulous man who twice changed sides in the civil war between Stephen and Matilda. In 1144 he and Stephen came to grips at Burwell Castle in Cambridgeshire, where he was shot in the head with an arrow. He was an excommunicate, but as he lay dying some Knights Templar happened by and clothed him in the habit of their order, with a red cross on the breast. They enclosed his corpse in a lead coffin and, for fear of the Church not daring to bury him, hung him on a tree in the orchard of the Old Temple at London.

*OS 166: TL 230026. Motte-and-bailey, 2 miles (3 km) north-west of Potters Bar, west of the A1(M) and B197. Not accessible without permission.*

## Sopwell Nunnery

According to Matthew Paris, the chronicler of St Albans Abbey, two devout women once lived here in a hut by the riverside, until the abbot of St Albans, hearing of their piety, provided them with a better dwelling place. This in time became Sopwell Nunnery, a small establishment of nuns following the Rule of St Benedict. While they lived in the hut, the two women used to dip their bread in a nearby spring, hence the name 'Sopwell'.

Later generations told a less innocent tale of Sopwell — that the nunnery and St Albans monastery, three-quarters of a mile apart on either side of the Ver, were connected by a secret passage that ran under the river, its purpose naturally scandalous.

*OS 166: TL 150064. South-east of St Albans Abbey, off Cottonmill Lane, close to the river. The surviving ruins are those of a house of about 1560-75, built on the same site.*

## Standon

Has Standon always been a place where archaic beliefs flourished? Here in Henry VIII's time a butcher was arraigned as a heretic for declaring that there was no god but the sun and the moon.

At the corner of the High Street and Paper Mill Lane stands a large chunk of puddingstone, rare in Hertfordshire and consequently much prized as a charm against the evil eye and witchcraft. The Hertfordshire name for such boulders, 'Plum Pudding Stones', describes them best, for they are lumps of glacial conglomerate, consisting of rounded flint pebbles (the plums) bound together in a silica matrix. They were set in much frequented places, such as gateways, and used as markers in churchyards. They were also known as 'mother stones'

because the pebbles were believed to be growing in them. It is said of a piece by Kingsbury Mill, in the parish of St Michael's, St Albans, that it will continue to grow as long as it stands.

*OS 166: TL 3922. Village 6 miles (10 km) west of Bishop's Stortford, off the A10 (Ermine Street) via the A120 (Standon Hill).*

# Standon Green End

In a field near Standon Green End a railed-in boulder commemorates the landing of Vincenzo Lunardi on 15th September 1784 after the first balloon voyage in England. Two hours previously, Lunardi, secretary to the Neapolitan ambassador, had taken off from Moorfields in London with a

*Standon Puddingstone (right), prized for its power to ward off the evil eye and witchcraft.*

*Henry Trigg's coffin (below) in the rafters in Stevenage Old Town.*

42

dog, a cat and a pigeon. The cold was intense, the dog felt faint, the cat even fainter, the pigeon simply left. Lunardi, bolstered by a couple of bottles of wine, no doubt expected a hero's welcome, but when he first touched down at North Mimms and called to some labourers to help him they said they would have nothing to do with the 'Devil's horse'. Elizabeth Brett, a servant-girl, was made of sterner stuff and caught hold of the rope he threw out, hanging on to it until some harvesters arrived. Lunardi rewarded her with five guineas and also asked her to take care of the cat until she saw him again. Throwing out some ballast, he, and presumably the dog, continued the journey, finally landing in the field where the 'Balloon Stone', as it is known, was erected to commemorate the occasion.

*OS 166: TL 3619. Location 4 miles (6 km) north of Ware, on the A10 (Ermine Street). Monument, TL 364198.*

## Stevenage (Old Town)

Fear of bodysnatchers may have prompted the extraordinary will of Henry Trigg, grocer and churchwarden of Stevenage. It is said that he was given a terrible fright when he stumbled on bodysnatchers late one night robbing a grave in the churchyard. Trigg owned a shop in the High Street, behind which was a cartshed, which he called his 'Hovel'. In his will, proved on 15th October 1724, he directed that his body be placed in its coffin in the 'Hovel', 'decently laid there upon a floor erected by my Executor, upon the purlin'. For more than two and a half centuries it has remained there, though Trigg's bones have been removed, some say by soldiers billeted there in the First World War who broke open the coffin and sold them as souvenirs. The coffin itself was repaired in about 1850 and the one that can be seen today may not be the original. That one should be there at all is astonishing, considering that 'Henry Trigg's House' later became the Castle (known as the Old

*The ascent of Vincenzo Lunardi on 15th September 1784.*

Castle) Inn and is now the National Westminster Bank.

*OS 166: TL 2325. 28 miles (45 km) north of London on the B197 (London Road). Henry Trigg's House is Number 37 High Street, the National Westminster Bank. Inside the bank is a wall display telling Trigg's story. There is free access to the barn in the parking area behind the building (along Middle Row, left up Baker Street, left again at end of street). It would be courteous to ask permission.*

## Temple Dinsley

The manor of Temple Dinsley was once the property of the Knights Templar, one of three orders founded during the Crusades to defend Jerusalem against the Infidel. They established a preceptory here in 1147 and remained until 1312, when their order was suppressed by the Pope. Dreadful accusations were levelled against them, particularly in regard to the rites observed at their midnight meetings.

*43*

Whether true or not, the rumours were widely believed and in the popular mind the Templars became synonymous with sorcery. No wonder that a subterranean passage, its mouth allegedly still visible at the beginning of the twentieth century, was rumoured to run from here to **Minsden Chapel**.

*OS 166: TL 1824. House (now a college) east of School Lane, Preston, 3 miles (5 km) south of Hitchin. The present building dates from 1714.*

# Tewin

In Tewin churchyard, nearly opposite the east end of the church, is the curious tomb of Lady Anne Grimston of Gorhambury, who died on 22nd November 1713. The story goes that she denied the dogma of the resurrection of the body and, as she lay dying, expressed the wish that, if it were true, trees might spring from her grave. In due course seven trees, ash and sycamore, did grow through her tomb.

Inside St Peter's Church, on the wall of the nave, is a tablet to Lady Cathcart, born Elizabeth Malyn in 1691, whose life story was the basis for a chapter in Maria Edgeworth's *Castle Rackrent* (1800). In rapid succession she married and buried three husbands, James Fleet, Colonel William Sabine and Lord Cathcart. Cathcart died in 1741 and this time she stayed a widow for more than four years. Then, at 54, she took a fancy to Lieutenant-Colonel Hugh Maguire of Castle Nugent, County Longford, in Ireland. Not long after the wedding she noticed on their morning drive that they were getting further and further from Tewin, and when she remarked on this her bridegroom revealed that he was carrying her off to Ireland. They were overtaken at Chester, but Maguire had bribed a maid to impersonate his wife and convince an attorney that she was going of her own free will. Once in Castle Nugent, he kept her a virtual prisoner for twenty years, whilst he squandered her fortune. In 1766 he was killed in a

duel and she returned to England, recovering her possessions through lawsuits. Of her marriages she remarked that the first was to please her parents, the second for money, the third for rank and the fourth because the Devil owed her a grudge. After the fourth, she is said to have had her wedding ring inscribed:

If I survive,
I will have five.

Yet she never did. She lived at Tewin House until her death at 97 and is said to have danced spiritedly at Welwyn Assembly when over eighty. She was buried at Tewin beside James Fleet, her first husband.

*OS 166: TL 2714. Village 4 miles (6 km) north-west of Hertford via the B1000 (Welwyn Road), Hertford Road. Gorhambury, TL 1107.*

# Theobalds Park

The eccentric entrance to Theobalds Park is Sir Christopher Wren's Temple Bar, first erected in Fleet Street in 1672, removed here from the City piece by piece and re-erected on its present site in 1888. The monument is very large, with a wide mid gateway for traffic flanked by narrow pedestrian footways.

*OS 166: TL 3400. Temple Bar, TL 344009. Just west of the A10 at Waltham Cross.*

# Thorley

In the nineteenth century the manor of Thorley was owned by the notorious hanging judge Lord Chief Justice Ellenborough. When in 1810 a bill was proposed in the House of Lords to abolish the death penalty for shoplifting, he opposed it on the grounds that no one would be able to leave his house for an hour without fearing that every stick of his property would be gone on his return. It is said that Ellenborough's own death was brought on by the shock of being contradicted by his jury, in the trial for blasphemy of William Hone in 1817.

*OS 167: TL 4718. Hamlet 2 miles (3 km) west of Bishop's Stortford via the B1004 (Great Hadham Road) and Thorley Lane.*

# Throcking

Sir Henry Chauncy in his *History of Hertfordshire* (1700) says that one irreligious lord of the manor of Throcking paved his kitchen with gravestones from the churchyard!

*OS 166: TL 3330. Village 2 miles (3 km) north-west of Buntingford.*

# Tring

There was once a castle where Tring Station now stands, the home in the time of Edward III of Sir Guy de Gravade. Like Faustus, Sir Guy sold his soul to the Devil in return for the Black Arts and some say that it was he who by magic made **Grim's Ditch**. Certainly it was by magic that he made himself rich, which tempted his servant, John Bond, to try his master's spells to fill his own pockets. Discovering the treachery, Sir Guy called on the Devil and with a clap of thunder and a flash of lightning the castle disappeared, its occupants with it. It returns every year on the anniversary of its destruction, and Sir Guy and John Bond can be seen about their wicked work.

*OS 165: SP 9211. 5 miles (8 km) north-west of Berkhamsted via the A41 (Tring Road). Tring Station (SP 950122) on Station Road from Tring to Aldbury.*

# Tyttenhanger

In the parish of Ridge is Tyttenhanger, a large brick mansion believed to have been built for Sir Henry Blount (1602-82) soon after 1654, possibly by the architect Peter Mills. Sir Henry, High Sheriff of Hertfordshire and a notable eccentric of the county,

was celebrated for his Levantine travels. John Evelyn mentions him in his *Diary* as 'the famous traveller and water-drinker', because in Turkey he had acquired the then unknown habit of drinking coffee. He still puts in an appearance at Tyttenhanger, clad in a satin dressing gown which rustles as he walks down the passage to his study on the second floor.

*OS 166: TL 1805. 2 miles (4 km) south-east of St Albans, via the A414 (Hatfield Road), the B6426 (Colney Heath Lane) and Barley Mow Lane. House, TL 193047, south-east of village, off the B556 (Coursers Road) from Colney Heath.*

# Wadesmill

The old Hertfordshire saying,

Ware and Wadesmill
Are worth all London

may not be entirely wishful thinking. There was a Roman settlement at Ware, where the bridge was of great strategic importance as the first crossing place of the river Lea north of London. At Wadesmill the Roman Ermine Street crossed the river Rib at a ford and further up the road there was a large Roman settlement at Puckeridge.

*OS 166: TL 3517. Village 2 miles (3 km) north of Ware. Puckeridge, TL 3823.*

# Walkern

In the early eighteenth century Jane Wenham, aged seventy, of Walkern was brought to trial for bewitching sixteen-year-old Ann Thorn. The Reverend Francis Bragge of Hitchin was a witness against her and afterwards wrote a pamphlet about the case which sold in great numbers. The charges against her included the claim that she shed no blood when pricked with a pin, that cats seemed unaccountably fond of her and that she could not repeat the Lord's Prayer. Impatient with this farrago of nonsense, the judge, Mr Justice Powell, tried to get her acquitted, but the jury insisted on convicting her. He was obliged to condemn her to death but made haste to intercede for her with Queen Anne, who granted a pardon. Jane Wenham died of old age at Hertingfordbury in 1730, the last person in England to have been condemned to death for witchcraft. The reality of the case against her may be judged by the fact that Ann Thorn stopped her accusations when her sweetheart came back and married her. The trial created a storm, leading to the 1735 Witchcraft Act abolishing the death penalty for witches.

Yet there were some strange goings-on at Walkern. The story goes that at Boxbury, now a deserted medieval village, the villagers decided to build a church in what was later known as Chapel Field. However, no sooner was the building begun, than the stones were mysteriously whisked through the air to the present site of St Mary's Church, Walkern. It was none other

*Waltham Cross marks one of the points at which the funeral cortège of Queen Eleanor halted for the night on its journey to London.*

than the Devil up to his tricks and as he moved the stones they heard him calling out, 'Walk-on! Walk-on!'

It was likewise a farmer of Walkern who, gloomily surveying his crops one wet summer, said he wished the Almighty would go to sleep for the six weeks until harvest. Quicker than thought, he himself fell into a sleep from which no one could waken him. Nor could men or horses shift him, so a shed was built over him where he lay, until the six weeks were up and in God's good time he awoke.

*OS 166: TL 2926. Village 4 miles (6 km) east of Stevenage on the B1037 (Stevenage Road/Walkern Road). Boxbury Farm, TL 2726.*

# Waltham Cross

Waltham Cross gets its name from its Eleanor Cross, one of twelve erected by Edward I along the route of his wife's funeral cortège from Harby in Nottinghamshire, where she died, to Westminster Abbey. The cross marks the point at which the procession turned aside in order to place the body in Waltham Abbey for the night. Work on it began in 1291, the year after Eleanor's death. Today's cross, nearly 50 feet tall, is shorter than the original, having had its upper tier removed in the eighteenth century, and its appearance owes much to restoration in 1833. Yet it remains, with the only other surviving Eleanor Crosses, at Northampton and Gedding-ton, a touching and romantic memorial to a departed queen.

*OS 166: TL 3500. South district of Cheshunt. Waltham Cross (TL 361004) in High Street. The original statues from the cross are now in Cheshunt Public Library.*

# Ware

Once housed in The Saracen's Head at Ware was the Great Bed of Ware, mentioned in Shakespeare's *Twelfth Night*. According to popular tradition, the bed was made by Jonas Fosbrooke,

*The Great Bed of Ware.*

a journeyman carpenter of Ware, who presented it to Edward IV in 1463. After the king's death the bed found its way back to Ware, where it was housed successively in different inns. Stoutly made of oak, 10 feet 10 inches long by 10 feet 7 inches wide, its exceptional size became even more exaggerated in travellers' tales: depending on who was telling the story, it could hold twelve or twenty couples, and 26 butchers and their wives had slept in it on the night King William III was crowned.

But the Great Bed acquired a bad name: those who lay in it got no sleep 'for the pinching, nipping, and scratching' that went on all night. This was generally thought to be the work of Jonas Fosbrooke, angry at the use his masterpiece was being put to. One Harrison Saxby, a Master of the Horse to Henry VIII, is said to have braved the terror of the bed in order to marry the girl he loved. She was the much courted daughter of a rich miller living at Chalk Island, near Ware, and Saxby swore he would do anything to win her. Hearing this as he passed through Ware, Henry summoned the girl and all her suitors and promised her hand

to the man who would endure a night in the Great Bed. The others promptly cried off, but Saxby accepted. Next morning he was found on the floor, more dead than alive and covered with bruises — but he got the girl.

Though the date 1463 which is painted on the headboard seems to prove the bed's 'history' true, it is actually Elizabethan. Expert opinion suggests that it always stood at Ware, having been made for The White Hart in around 1590 as an advertising gimmick. After that it moved from inn to inn: The George, The Crown and finally to The Saracen's Head, where it remained until 1870, when it was sold to the owner of the Rye House Hotel, Hoddesdon, Charles Dickens having already tried to buy it. Eventually, in 1931, it was acquired by the Victoria and Albert Museum in London, where in all its grossness it can still be seen.

In the 1760s John Scott of Amwell House, poet and liberal thinker, built himself a fashionable Gothick folly, a place, in his own words:

Where midst thick oaks the subterranean way
To the arched Grot admits a feeble ray,
Where glossy pebbles pave the varied floors,

47

*A warrior is said to be asleep in Wayting Hill until he is called to battle again.*

And rough flint walls are decked with
shells and ores,
And silvery pearls, spread o'er the roof on
high,
Glimmer like faint stars in a twilight sky.
From noon's fierce glare, perhaps he
pleased retires,
Indulging musings which the place in-
spires.

Winding passages tunnelling into the hillside link the six chambers of his grotto, which was described by Dr Johnson as a 'Fairy Hall'. On the hill above is another favourite spot, a belvedere or gazebo.

*OS 166: TL 3514. 21 miles (33 km) north of London on the A1170. Scott's Grotto is in Scott's Road west of Ware College (TL 358139). Open mainly by appointment, telephone: 0920 464131.*

In the 1930s there was certainly an oblong bare patch there, just the size of a grave, but the sceptical point out that the soil here is porous chalk.

In the nineteenth century people would travel for miles to see one of the wonders of Hertfordshire, the celebrated Fig Tree Tomb in the grave-yard of the parish church of St Mary. According to local report, it was the tomb of Ben Wangford, who lived around the end of the eighteenth century. He did not believe in a hereafter and so arranged that, when he was buried, something would be placed with his remains that would grow as a sign to his relations if his soul indeed survived. In due course a fig tree grew out of the tomb, proving that Ben was wrong and there was an afterlife.

# Watford

Tradition says that Tommy Deacon of Wiggen Hall, Watford, gave his name to Deacons Hill by riding his horse so recklessly down it for a wager that he broke his neck and was buried at its foot at the crossroads. According to another story, however, his grave is at the top of the hill and is always dry even in the wettest weather.

*OS 166: TQ 1196. 16 miles (26 km) north-west of London off the M1. Deacons Hill runs between Wiggenhall Road (A4178) and Eastbury Road (A4125). St Mary's Church is in Church Street, in the town centre. The Fig Tree Tomb is still there, on the south side of the chancel, but the fig tree died a couple of decades ago, and the inscription is illegible.*

# Wayting Hill

Wayting Hill, near the hillfort of Ravensburgh Castle, Hexton, is a round barrow in which a warrior lies asleep, waiting until the day when he can arise and march to victory.

On Hock Monday (the second after Easter) men and women used to go together to the top of Wayting Hill, whence the women would try to pull an ash pole to the bottom, while the men did their best to keep it at the top. This curious custom, which lasted to the reign of Elizabeth I, ostensibly celebrated the end of the Danish occupation (Ravensburgh was locally believed to be a Danish fort.) Whilst it was taking place money was collected to repair the church and bells, and it may be that an old pagan ceremony was given a new Christian occasion and purpose.

*OS 166: TL 0930. In the Barton Hills, immediately south of the B655 from Barton-le-Clay, via Hexton and Pegsdon, to Hitchin.*

# Welwyn

To relieve his people from the burden of the Danes, Ethelred the Unready sent out word in the year 1002 that at a certain hour on the feast of St Brice (13th November) all the Danes in the kingdom should be massacred. So much is history. Popular tradition adds that the Massacre of St Brice's Day began at Welwyn, hence its name, because the 'weal' (as in 'welfare') of England began there.

In the parish church of St Mary, on the west wall of the north aisle, is a memorial tablet to Edward Young, rector here from 1730 to his death on 5th April 1765. He lived in a house by the river, the present Guessens. Witty, worldly, with a passion for bowls (he constructed a bowling green at Welwyn and haunts another at **Hitchin**), he is nevertheless best known for his elegiac poem *Night Thoughts* (1742), occasioned by the death of his wife, with its well known sentiment 'Procrastination is the thief of time'. It is his melancholy and not his sporting vein that is remembered too by the sombre, maroon-purple moss rose that commemorates him, Nuits de Young.

*OS 166: TL 2316. 5 miles (8 km) south of Stevenage, off the A1(M). Nuits de Young can be seen in the Gardens of the Rose (Royal National Rose Society), Chiswell Green, St Albans. Off the B4630 (Watford Road).*

# Weston

On your left as you enter Weston

*Jack o' Legs' 14 foot grave in Weston churchyard.*

49

*The seamy side of Stanley family history is said to be represented in the sign of The Eagle and Child at Whitwell (above) and the Bull Inn (left) was haunted by the ghost of a recruiting officer.*

churchyard, two stones 14 feet apart reputedly mark the grave of Jack o' Legs, the Weston giant. According to the earliest version of his story, he was a robber who lived in a wood hereabouts and, like Robin Hood, plundered the rich to feed the poor. Eventually the Baldock bakers, from whom he used to steal bread, caught him and hanged him. As his last request he asked for a bow to be put in his hand and fired an arrow, asking to be buried where it fell. This happened to be in Weston churchyard.

Jack's Hill, a mile north of Graveley on the old Great North Road, was supposed to be where he watched out for wealthy travellers and, until it was filled in in the nineteenth century, there was a 'Jack's Cave' where he hid his loot. Visitors would come from afar to see Jack's grave and for a tip the parish clerks of Weston would produce a huge bone they maintained was his thighbone. In the seventeenth century, it was sold to the gardener John Tradescant (probably the Elder, who worked at **Hatfield House**), eventually finding its way to Oxford's Ashmolean Museum, where it was lost.

*OS 166: TL 2630. Village 3 miles (4 km) south-east of Baldock via the A507 (Clothall Road) and Ashanger Lane. Jack's Hill, TL 2329, east of the B197 (North Road), 1 mile (2 km) north of Graveley.*

# Whitwell

The Maiden's Head has often led Young people in to sin.

Not very appropriate, one might think, to The Maiden's Head, Whitwell, which has on its sign the head of Elizabeth I, the Virgin Queen. But this old inn name originally referred to the heraldic crest of Catherine Parr, the Dukes of Buckingham and the Mercers' Company — the Maidenhead.

Further along the street, The Eagle and Child bears the date 1747, but the back of the building is older. The Eagle and Child is the badge of the Stanleys, the Earls of Derby. The story goes that their ancestor, Sir Thomas Latham, had his illegitimate son placed at the foot of a tree in which an eagle was nesting. Out walking with his wife, he pretended to find the child and persuaded her to adopt it as their heir. When later he changed his mind, the family altered his eagle crest to one of an eagle preying upon a child. The Whitwell pub was probably so called because the Stanleys briefly held the neighbouring manor of Stagenhoe, granted in 1488 to Thomas Stanley, first Earl of Derby.

The medieval Bull Inn used to be troubled by a ghost, reputedly that of a recruiting officer from the time of the Napoleonic Wars who had been done to death there. His skeleton is said to have been found in the 1930s in a walled-up cupboard on the first floor and to have been buried in the churchyard, since when the ghost has been at rest.

It was said at Whitwell around 1900 that, if you got up before dawn and strolled quietly towards Bendish and Breachwood Green, you would hear a phantom woodman at work. Yet however quickly you entered the thicket from which the sound seemed to come, by the time you arrived no one would be there.

*OS 166: TL 1821. Village 4 miles (7 km) north-west of Welwyn via the B656 (Codicote Road) and then the B651 from Codicote. Stagenhoe, TL 1822. Bendish, TL 1621.*

# Index

*Page numbers in italic refer to illustrations*